Floyd FOOD

C000179817

A.

Published by Absolute Press
Scarborough House, 29 James Street West, Bath, BA1 2BT

First printed October 1981
Reprinted June 1982
Reprinted October 1987
Reprinted October 2009

© Keith Floyd 1981

General Editor **Jon Croft**

The publishers would like to thank Sarah Croft and Paula Borton for their
invaluable help and assistance in the editing of this book.

Illustrations and design
Carl Willson MSIAD

Cover Photograph
Mike Cooper (Ken James Photographic Ltd, Bristol)

Printed and bound by
William Clowes Ltd, Copland Way, Ellough Beccles, Suffolk NR34 7TL

All rights reserved. No part of this publication may be reproduced, stored
in a retrieval system or transmitted in any form or by any means, electronic,
mechanical, photocopying, recording or otherwise without the prior
permission of Absolute Press.

For Julie, Patrick, Mum and Dad. With love.

Contents

Foreword

"What about lunch, Pat?" I said. We were making a television film in Bristol, my favourite city, and as we were to be there for more than three weeks catering arrangements were going to be important. Normally a film unit is fed by strange men who follow you around in a small lorry. "Ah," said Pat Dromgoole our director, "we're going to Keith Floyd's in Clifton." This was in the early 1970s. The first meal was so good that afterwards I remember saying to Pat, "never mind the filming, let's just make sure Keith can fit us in every day."

From that time on whenever I have visited Bristol a meal at one of Keith's restaurants is a pleasure to which I have always looked forward. Obviously his food is good or I wouldn't be writing this, but above all there is always that one essential quality, you are made to feel that the meal you are having is Keith's most important job that day. I can think of no higher praise. This book is bound to be good.

Introduction

This book is intended to enable all those who are interested in good food to produce uncomplicated but tasty dishes without going frantic. All the recipes have been carefully conceived so that your life in the kitchen is not one of hectic pan surveillance and unnecessary and elaborate presentation – in fact two-thirds of the recipes in the book can be cooked in one pan. Basically 'Floyd's Food' is a guide to the way that thousands of untrained and trained cooks prepare their meals throughout France; very ordinary people who may never have read a cookery book in their lives but who can provide outstandingly delicious meals at the drop of a hat. Their philosophy and mine is that cooking is fun, eating is fun and that snobbery plays no part.

Many of the recipes included in this book are original, whilst many others are basic classics adapted by me to put them within the reach of the home cook. They all have in common a certain simplicity – the simplicity of the cooking of Provincial France.

I lived and worked in the Vaucluse in Provence for four years where I ran my own restaurant – 'Floyd's'. The restaurant scene in France and in particular around Provence is one of infinite variety. The best are quite marvellous; the elegant 'Hiely' in Avignon which serves exquisite food with great style, dignity and lack of pretension; or 'Les Geraniens' at Les Beaumettes which serves mountainous and deliciously tangy local dishes, like Civet de Lièvre (the hare shot by the patron) or brochette of grives at Christmas time accompanied by gallons of rosé for the price of a bottle of plonk at your local trattoria. And then, as everywhere in the world, there are the bad – the pizzerias and the little 'restos' where they charge like wounded buffalo and no doubt cut the 'steak frites' from the very same beast.

But to return to my own restaurant. When it was first opened I found to my surprise that I had very little trouble in attracting customers. They came in Gallic droves to eat 'fish with jam', lamb with mint, le pudding and to laugh. They came out of curiosity, blatantly expecting the worst and left saying 'pas mal', which I promise you is one of the highest compliments a Frenchman can pay. Once they had discovered that the English did not eat jam with fish and that I was offering 'pas mal' French Cuisine the battle was virtually won. There was however one final skirmish. I had completely overlooked the regional obsession of the French – that obsession that makes it impossible for the natives of Bordeaux to acknowledge the wine of the Côte d'Or and vice versa. To my amazement I found that I knew more of French dishes than did my customers. The people of the Midi were simply not familiar with the cooking of Normandy. Often I would be called to the table and told "c'est bon, mais c'est pas Français" – by 'Français', of course, they meant Provençal. It will probably come as no surprise to learn that much of the inspiration for this book came from the years spent in Provence.

I hope that the recipes that follow will allow you to enjoy your own cooking at the same time as your guests and family. 'Floyd's Food' is intended to release you not to enslave.

I would like to thank, Peter Gardiner, John F. Marshall, Michael McGowan, Mike Dowdswell, Douglas Bullock, Malcolm Thomas, Ken Pickard, Leonard Rossiter and all my customers.
Allez les pommes de terre!

Botticelli isn't a wine, you juggins! Botticelli's a cheese!
(Punch 1894)

 This symbol appears alongside all those recipes that can be cooked in one pan.

Sauces

Aioli
Rouille
Mayonnaise
Hollandaise Sauce
Mustard Sauce
Béarnaise Sauce
Tartare Sauce
Béchamel Sauce
Tomato Sauce
Onion Marmalade
Onion Sauce
Herb Flavoured Butters

All the sauces in this section are excellent and easy to make. They make smashing accompaniments to many of the dishes in the book – for example, 'aioli' with the 'quickest fish terrine in the world' or the marvellously versatile 'tomato sauce' with the 'chicken liver mousse'. Try to become used to making them for they require very little effort and result in terrific effect.

Aioli

8 cloves garlic
3 egg yolks
⅓ litre olive oil
1 tablespoon lemon juice
salt and pepper

This is the quick way to make this excellent sauce.
Put the garlic, lemon juice and olive oil in the liquidizer and whizz until the garlic is puréed with the oil.

Then using a hand whisk, beat the egg yolks in a mixing bowl into a froth. Still beating, drip in evenly the garlic oil slowly until it thickens like mayonnaise. Season with salt and pepper.

Rouille

2 cloves garlic
1 oz. ball damp breadcrumbs
¼ teaspoon Spanish cayenne (hot)
4 fl. oz. olive oil

This is my quick version of the classic hot sauce for bouillabaisse, fish soup etc.
Put the garlic, breadcrumbs and cayenne into the liquidizer and whizz, dripping in the oil until the appearance reaches that of a red mayonnaise.

Mayonnaise

3 egg yolks
12 fl. oz. best olive oil
1 teaspoon mild mustard
juice 1 lemon
salt and pepper

Remember, eggs and oil must be of same room temperature or else disaster!
Beat the egg yolks until frothy. Continue beating whilst dripping in the olive oil. When thick, mix in the lemon juice and mustard and season with salt and pepper.

Hollandaise Sauce

½ lb. melted clarified unsalted butter
3 egg yolks
juice 1 lemon
salt and pepper

Beat the eggs thoroughly in a mixing bowl. Then, still beating, add the melted butter drop by drop. Continue beating until you have a thin custard consistency. Add the lemon juice and salt and pepper.

Serve at once from a separate jug directly onto the food. Avoid very hot plates as the sauce may melt.

Mustard Sauce

To make mustard sauce all you do is add a teaspoon or two of fine French mustard to hollandaise sauce. Check the seasoning as it may need more salt, pepper and lemon juice. Easy, isn't it.

Béarnaise Sauce

3 or 4 egg yolks
½ lb. unsalted butter
2 tablespoons wine vinegar
1 finely chopped shallot or small onion
½ glass white wine
pepper
1 teaspoon tarragon leaves or dried tarragon

You can flavour the basic egg yolk and butter sauce any way that you want. For instance just add chopped mint instead of tarragon when serving lamb.

Melt the butter and keep hot.

Boil the wine and vinegar with the shallot and pepper (and also the tarragon if using dried) until reduced by half.

In a bowl, whisk the egg yolks. Reduce speed of the whisk and pour the butter in slowly, whisking all the while. Pop in the fresh tarragon and then whisk in the reduced wine/vinegar mix.

Serve with steak or other grilled meats, also with the 'stuffed deep fried mushrooms' recipe on page 24.

Tartare Sauce

1 cup mayonnaise
1 tablespoon chopped capers
1 teaspoon chopped tarragon
1 teaspoon chopped shallot
pinch chopped parsley

Mix the above into the mayonnaise – *et voilà!*

Béchamel Sauce

½ pint milk
2 oz. butter
2 tablespoons fine flour
1 bay leaf
parsley stalk
1 onion ring
sliver of carrot
salt and pepper

In a pan, heat the milk gently with the salt and pepper, herbs and vegetables. Leave to stand for 15 minutes.

In another pan melt the butter and stir in the flour. Allow to cook for a minute or so without browning.

Strain the milk and, stirring all the while, pour into the melted butter. Cook over a low heat for 10 minutes.

You can enrich it with cream.

You can put chopped parsley in it.

You can put grated cheese in it.

You can also use it to make the 'ham and lettuce with cheese' recipe on page 63.

It's a very useful sauce.

Tomato Sauce

14 oz. tin tomatoes
2 cloves garlic, chopped
1 medium onion, finely chopped
1 teaspoon fresh or dried basil
1 tablespoon chopped parsley
1 level tablespoon white sugar
1 tablespoon olive oil
lots of black pepper

Fry the onions and garlic in the olive oil until soft.

When soft, add all the other ingredients and cook over a low heat for 15 minutes.

And then liquidize the lot. This sauce can be served either hot or cold.

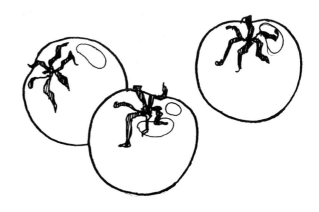

Onion Marmalade

4 lb. onions, cut into very fine rings
2 tablespoons of the blandest cooking oil
1 cup caster sugar
1 wine glass sherry vinegar
lots of black pepper

This sauce is superb with grilled lamb or game. Or even a grilled poussin. Make a lot because it keeps well.

Fry the onions in the oil with lots of black pepper until they turn golden but not burnt. Add the sugar and vinegar and continue cooking until the onions begin to caramelise or get sticky and solid like jam – about 45 minutes. Serve hot.

Onion Sauce

½ lb. finely sliced onions
2 oz. butter
1 tablespoon flour
¼ pint milk, at least – warmed
1 tablespoon cream
salt, pepper and nutmeg

Fry the onions in butter until they are soft but not burnt or coloured.

Add the flour and stir in. Now add the warmed milk and season with salt, pepper and nutmeg. Cook for a few minutes, stirring to avoid lumps. When the sauce thickens whizz it through the liquidizer with the cream.

Serve warm with lamb or even a fried egg.

Herb Flavoured Butters

It's very nice to have a pat of herb flavoured butter gently melting over a piece of grilled meat or fish and as the procedure is so straightforward I fully recommend that you keep some handy. Floyd has spoken!

Of course, use fresh herbs whenever possible. Just chop them very finely and mix with softened butter. Then place on a piece of greaseproof paper and roll up into a sausage shape. Cut off as required – it will freeze well.

Some examples:

garlic and parsley	– steak or fish
shallot	– fish
chives and mint	– lamb
rosemary and thyme	– pork

or just mix in anchovy paste or some puréed prawns for grilled fish.

Starters

French Onion Soup
Provençale Vegetable Soup
Watercress Express
Frozen Sardines
The Quickest Fish Terrine in the World
Stuffed Mussels Provençale
Gratin of Mussels
Chicken Liver Mousse
Cold Ham Soufflé
Hot Onion Tart
Red Pepper Mousse
Greek Mushrooms
Stuffed Deep Fried Mushrooms

Here is a short selection of starters which are
easy to prepare and serve and which will set any
meal off on a high note.

French Onion Soup
Serves 6-8

4 lb. onions, finely sliced
2 pints red plonk
2 pints water
1 tablespoon tomato purée
black pepper
4 oz. butter
1 tablespoon flour
1 meat stock cube
1 bay leaf
1 tablespoon fresh chopped parsley
4 oz. gruyère
4 slices stale French bread to make croutons

This unfortunate soup has been murdered by countless aspiring gastronauts in the bistros of our land (in France a bistro sells only drink – possibly a sandwich). This is how it should be done, except for the addition of a stock cube, but then we are not concerned with lengthy stock making in this book.

Brown the onions in butter. Allow some of them to burn i.e. caramelise. Add the flour and allow to brown. Add all the other ingredients and cook slowly for 1 or 2 hours or until the volume has reduced by ¼.

Make the croutons and place on top of the soup in individual fireproof dishes. Sprinkle with the gruyère. Pop under the grill to melt the cheese and serve.

Provençale Vegetable Soup
Serves 6-8

1 onion, diced
1 carrot, diced
4 cloves garlic, chopped
1 lb. green beans, chopped
4 raw potatoes, diced
6 tomatoes, chopped

1 tablespoon tomato purée
4 oz. small vermicelli or spaghetti broken into pieces ¼" long
4 or 5 pints water
1 lb. shelled broad beans
4 tablespoons fresh finely chopped basil mixed with 4 cloves
   crushed garlic and some olive oil to make a paste
1 dish grated Parmesan cheese

Put all the ingredients except the vermicelli, paste and cheese into
a large saucepan and cook until the vegetables are tender. Then
add the vermicelli and continue cooking for another 10 minutes or
so. Stir in the paste and cook for a further 5 minutes.

Serve with Parmesan cheese sprinkled liberally over this
Provençale form of the Italian 'minestrone'.

Watercress Express
Serves 4

4 oz. watercress
2 tablespoons instant potato mix
pinch nutmeg
2 tablespoons double cream
1 chicken stock cube
2 pints milk
pepper but no salt because of the stock cube

Pop the lot into the liquidizer for a revolution or two and then heat
gently in a pan. Simmer for 5 minutes and . . . voilà!

*To think of all the marvellous ways they are using liquidizers
nowadays it makes a fellow proud to be a cook.*

Frozen Sardines

sardines
plenty of lemon pieces
salt
mixed herbs (herbes de provence)

Defrost the sardines gently and dry very carefully.

The sardines are oily and will need no extra fat for cooking. So, preheat the grill, sprinkle the fish with plenty of salt and your herbs. Cook for 3 minutes each side until the skin is charred a little. Serve with your lemon pieces and bread and butter.

The Quickest Fish Terrine in the World
Serves 4-6

approx. 5 oz. very firm white fish – monkfish is ideal
8 fillets sole
1 tablespoon chopped parsley
1 sachet aspic jelly
2 tablespoons double cream
1 egg yolk
1 whole egg
2 oz. watercress
juice ½ lemon
pinch dried tarragon
small knob butter
salt and pepper

I suppose you would have to call this a true 'Basse Cuisine' recipe. But it works and tastes good. When you can do this one with ease then you can have a go at Michel Guerard's.

Chop the monkfish into small cubes.

Put the monkfish, parsley, tarragon, watercress, egg and yolk, cream, salt and pepper into the liquidizer. Whizz until you have a smooth green paste.

Meanwhile lay 4 of the sole fillets into a terrine and season with the lemon juice, salt and pepper. Pour the paste from the liquidizer over the fish and cover with the remaining fillets. Season again with lemon juice, salt and pepper. Cover with a piece of buttered greaseproof paper.

Place the terrine in a tray with water in it and pop into the oven at 180°C/350°F/gas 4 for about 45 minutes. Check the terrine from time to time – it should rise and come away from the sides when cooked.

Allow to cool and strain off any excess liquid. Prepare aspic and pour over the terrine. Allow to set. Serve with either our sauce Rouille or Aioli.

Stuffed Mussels Provençale
Serves 4

4 pints mussels
2 glasses white wine
4 oz. breadcrumbs
1 cup our tomato sauce – page 12
2 tablespoons cream
2 oz. butter
1 onion, finely chopped
2 cloves garlic, chopped
chopped parsley

Wash and scrape the mussels.

Cook the mussels in a shallow pan in the white wine until they open. Save the juice. Remove the empty shell from each mussel and discard. Place the filled shells on a grilling tray.

In another pan melt the butter and add the onions, garlic and parsley and cook for 2 to 3 minutes until soft.

Add the tomato sauce, cream and juices saved from the mussels and bubble for a moment or two. Stir in breadcrumbs. Turn off the gas and allow the breadcrumbs to soak up all the mouthwatering juices.

Stuff each mussel shell with the mixture and put under a hot grill until they turn golden.

Gratin of Mussels
Serves 4

4 pints mussels
4 oz. fresh breadcrumbs
4 oz. double cream
2 oz. grated Parmesan cheese
1 onion, very finely chopped
2 oz. butter
2 glasses white wine
pepper
parsley

Wash and scrape the mussels.

Cook the mussels in a shallow pan in the white wine until they open. Save the juice.

Retain those halves of the shells containing the mussels. Lay them on a grilling tray.

In another pan melt the butter, add the onions and cook for 2 or 3 minutes until soft. Add the parsley, the juice from the mussels, the cream and the cheese. Bubble for a moment or two and then stir in the breadcrumbs. Turn off the gas and allow the breadcrumbs to soak up the juice.

Now stuff each mussel shell with the mixture and pop them under the grill until they turn golden.

Chicken Liver Mousse
Serves 10

1 lb. chicken livers
1 clove chopped garlic
1 teaspoon chopped parsley
1 teaspoon thyme
½ finely chopped onion
1 tablespoon tomato purée
measure brandy
2 oz. butter

¼ pint double cream
5 stiffly beaten egg whites
1 oz. sachet of aspic (to 8 fl. oz. water)
pepper and salt

Make sure that the livers are dry.

Fry the livers in hot butter with the onion, garlic and thyme for 10 minutes. Pour over brandy and flame.

Add the parsley, tomato purée and salt and pepper. Cook for a further 5 minutes. Allow to cool.

When cool, liquidize the lot and add the cream and aspic. Leave until it begins to set, then fold in the egg whites.

Serve with cold tomato sauce – page 12.

Cold Ham Soufflé
Serves 8

1 lb. cooked ham, chopped
½/¾ pint double cream
2 oz. packet powdered aspic, dissolved in ½ pint water
black pepper
6 stiffly beaten egg whites

Liquidize the ham with the cream and ground black pepper to taste.

Make up aspic jelly as to instructions on packet and allow to cool, then add to the ham mixture. As it begins to set fold in the stiffly beaten egg whites. Pour into a suitable sized mould and allow to set.

Serve with a crisp salad.

Hot Onion Tart
Serves 4

4 individual tart cases, 3" in diameter
flaky pastry
2 large, finely sliced onions
2 large eggs
4 tablespoons double cream
2 oz. butter
8 anchovy fillets
salt and pepper

Melt the butter in a frying pan and throw in the onion slices, turning them soft and transparent.

Roll out the pastry and line the tins.

Next beat the eggs and cream together and season with salt and pepper. Mix the onions in and fill the cases. Bake in a hot oven, 220°C/425°F/gas 7 for about 15 minutes.

Decorate with anchovy fillets and eat them before they deflate.

If you want to eat them cold, add a slice of hardboiled egg, a black olive and a slice of tomato to each one and you will have an exact replica of a pissaladière as served by the best baker in Aix en Provence. He also makes the best marrons glacés in the world but his croissants are lousy.

Red Pepper Mousse
Serves 4-6

2 large ripe red peppers
4 egg whites, stiffly whisked
1 packet aspic powder
1 tablespoon tomato purée
pinch thyme
dash chilli sauce
5 tablespoons double cream
salt and pepper
some of our tomato sauce – page 12

Prepare ¼ pint aspic jelly by following instructions on packet except make it to double strength. Do not allow to set.

Cook the peppers in salted boiling water for 20 minutes or so until tender. Drain, cut out the pith and chop into small pieces.

Now put everything except the egg whites and tomato sauce into the liquidizer and whizz for a few seconds. Leave to cool.

Just before the purée sets, fold in the egg whites, mixing thoroughly. Check seasoning and pour into wine glasses or ramekins. Chill well. Serve with a spoonful of cold tomato sauce.

Greek Mushrooms
Serves 4-6

1 lb. small button mushrooms
4 tablespoons olive oil
1 tablespoon sherry vinegar
1 tablespoon coriander seeds, coarsely crushed
1 bay leaf
½ lemon cut in very, very thin slices
1 tablespoon chopped parsley
½ tin tomatoes and their juice
salt and pepper

Wash and dry the mushrooms. Salt and pepper them.

In a pan heat the olive oil and vinegar with the coriander seeds. When hot drop in everything else including the mushrooms and cook wildly for 5 or 6 minutes.

Lift out the mushrooms and allow the sauce to reduce by half. Pour back over the mushrooms. Chill for ages and eat them later.

Stuffed Deep Fried Mushrooms
Serves 4

1 lb. large button mushrooms
few ounces of our chicken liver mousse saved from the last
  soirée
fresh breadcrumbs
cooking oil
little flour
1 egg and ½ cup milk, beaten together

*The stalks from the mushrooms should be saved for soup
tomorrow: i.e. boil them in milk with salt, pepper and nutmeg;
liquidize and add double cream – serve.*

Stuff the caps of the mushrooms with the mousse but don't fill
them above the level of the rim.

Dust them in flour and dip in the egg mix. Then roll them in
breadcrumbs.

Heat the oil to hot and drop them in. Fry gently for about 5
minutes.

Strain the fat completely off them and serve with hollandaise or
béarnaise sauce – pages 9 and 10.

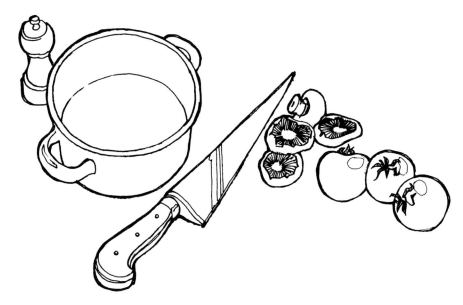

Fish

Simple Fish Stock

Simple Flat Fish

A Simple Fish Stew that Reminds You
of France

The Only Way To Cook A Lobster

The Only Way To Cook A Crayfish

Langoustines Sauce Rouge à la Floyd

Unidentified Frozen Fish in Envelopes

Fish Tart for Gourmets with Lemon Sauce

Bass with Pernod

Carp, Eel or Pike in Red Wine

Cod Cutlets with Aioli

Monkfish with Paprika Sauce

Monkfish Roasted with Bacon and Garlic

Monkfish with Cream and Brandy

Grey Mullet with Mustard

Scallops on a Skewer with Cointreau

Scallops on a Skewer with Pernod

Baked Trout with Hollandaise Sauce

Salmon Escalopes with Watercress

Whenever possible use fresh fish. When in the
fishmonger don't be afraid to ask to feel and
smell the fish and insist on having it cut to the
size that YOU want. If, as in the case of
langoustines, you are forced to buy frozen ensure
that you defrost very gently. Always, whether
frozen or fresh, dry the fish very carefully before
cooking.

You will find that shellfish, such as scallops, taste
much better if they are slightly underdone. In fact
no fish should be overcooked.

Simple Fish Stock

1 finely sliced onion
1 bay leaf
1 large sprig parsley
½ leek, finely sliced
1 fish head
2 or 3 sole or other fish bones

Cover all with cold water and bring to the boil. Simmer gently for 30 minutes so that the liquid remains clear. Leave to cool before using.

Simple Flat Fish

This is a basic guide to cooking flat fish such as plaice, Dover sole, lemon sole etc., in a simple and delicious way.

Golden rules:

1 Skin both sides of the fish and trim fins.
2 Have the grill very, very hot.
3 If frozen, ensure that the fish is completely defrosted and dry.
4 Have plenty of lemon around and also a good home made mayonnaise based sauce, such as tartare – page 11.
5 To cook: season your fish with salt and pepper and lemon juice. Preheat the grilling tray and melt a little butter on it to prevent the fish from sticking. Grill the fish for about 6 minutes each side, turning only once. Serve with your sauce, home-made chips, a crisp green salad and the best white wine you can afford.

A Simple Fish Stew that Reminds You of France
Serves 4-6

fillets of all or some of bass, red snapper, bream, conger eel
   and cod – quantity to preference
1 pint aioli – page 8
4 oz. double cream
6 toasted croutons, covered in sauce Rouille – page 8
4 pints fish stock – page 26
2 lb. boiled potatoes
fennel fern
salt and pepper

Dry and season the fillets of fish and poach them gently in the 4
pints of fish stock. Remove and place in a warm shallow bowl
with the boiled potatoes.

Take half of the stock, add the double cream and heat through,
stirring all the while. Then whisk in the aioli slowly over a low
heat and cook until the consistency of thin custard is obtained –
remove at once from heat.

Pour the sauce liberally over the fish and potatoes and float the
rouille covered croutons in the sauce. Strew fronds of fennel over
the lot and serve the beautiful yellow dish with its red floating
islands at once – with lots of iced white Rhone wine.

The Only Way to Cook a Lobster
for 2 people or less

1 live 4 lb. lobster – dead will do if you have a squeamish
   nature
½ lb. unsalted butter
2 whole lemons cut into halves
salt and pepper
1 bottle Le Montrachet to be drunk with the lobster

Place a large knife in the back of the lobster's head. Plunge it
quickly into the head and pull it back cutting the fish completely in

half. The movements are purely reaction. *The beast is dead!* Remove the dark sac from the head.

Squeeze the lemons over the flesh and season with salt and pepper. Liberally cover with butter and place under a hot grill until the shell turns pink and the flesh is cooked – about 20 minutes.

Remove the fish to a polished table beset with fine glass ware and silver cutlery. If dining alone a faint smile of satisfaction is permitted as you pour your wine.

The Only Way to Cook a Crayfish

Exactly as above although you are permitted to try a vintage Hermitage instead of the Le Montrachet!

Langoustines Sauce Rouge à la Floyd
Serves 2 or 4

1 kilo box langoustines

1 cup our tomato sauce – page 12

1 coffeespoon chilli or other hot sauce – not filled to overflowing

1 tablespoon finely chopped onions

1 clove garlic, finely chopped

1 tablespoon parsley, finely chopped

1 teaspoon herbes de Provence (mixed herbs)

2 tablespoons olive oil

1 large measure cooking brandy, eau de vie or Armagnac

½ glass dry white wine

salt and black pepper

You can order these prawns from your fishmonger. Langoustines are perhaps better known as scampi in this country. However I do mean you to buy the whole beast, shell and all, not a packet of scampi tails. They come in kilo boxes from Scotland and one box makes an excellent meal for 2 or a superb starter for 4.

Use a large diameter, heavy frying pan so that all the beasts are in contact with the heat at the same time. Fry the onions and garlic in olive oil until they are soft. Add the langoustines, herbes de Provence and parsley and fry gently for 5 minutes. Add a pinch of salt and a few turns of the pepper mill.

Now pour in the spirit and flame. When the flames are out add the white wine and allow to bubble for 2 minutes or less to reduce a little. Add the tomato and the chilli sauces and stir and simmer for another 2 or 3 minutes.

Serve with finger bowls and lots of napkins, one of which should be well tucked into the collar of your St. Laurent silk shirt.

Unidentified Frozen Fish in Envelopes
Serves 6

6 frozen haddock or hake portions
tin foil for the envelopes
chopped parsley in butter
finely sliced mushrooms – 6 fine slices each envelope
6 thin rounds lemon
6 oz. double cream
1 measure Pernod

For the busy gastronaut with no conscience this is a winner.

Cut out 6 rectangles of tin foil 12" × 10" and place a fish in the centre of each. Divide the other ingredients equally between the envelopes and seal, taking care that the liquid cannot escape.

Pop the envelopes in the oven at 200°C/400°F/gas 6 for 20 minutes.

Serve with matchstick chips and a bottle of unknown wine recently discovered by one of the more trendy wine columnists.

Fish Tart for Gourmets with Lemon Sauce
Serves 4

12 oz. Dover sole fillets
6 large scallops cut in rounds $\frac{1}{4}$" thick
10 oz. flaky pastry – puff will do

For the stuffing:
2 oz. watercress
1 whole egg
1 yolk
4 oz. fillet white fish
salt and pepper

For the sauce:
3 eggs
juice 2 lemons
little salt to taste

Line a 9" shallow sided tart dish with pastry and reserve the rest
for the lid.

Liquidize all the stuffing ingredients until stiff and smooth.

Season the Dover sole and the scallops and line the base of the
dish with half the fish. Then spread the stuffing over the fish and
cover with the remainder of the fillets. Cover the tart with the rest
of the pastry and brush with beaten egg or milk. Bake in the oven
at 200°C/400°F/gas 6 for 20 minutes.

Before serving, whisk the eggs and the lemon juice in a double
saucepan until a frothy sauce materialises. Add a little salt to
taste. Cut the tart like a cake, mask with lemon sauce and serve a
separate dish of mange tout or green beans. A good Macon or
white Rhone goes well.

Bass with Pernod
Serves 6

6 bass steaks or fillets from a big fish
seasoned flour
juice 1 lemon
1 measure Pernod
4 oz. butter
1 finely chopped shallot or ½ small onion
8 oz. double cream
12 green peppercorns, preferably soaked
chopped parsley for garnishing

Dredge the fish in flour and knock off excess.

Fry the fish gently in the butter with the shallot for about 3 minutes each side. Add the Pernod and flame it over the fish – before the flames extinguish pour over the cream. Add the peppercorns, lemon juice and adjust the seasoning. Bubble for a moment or two. Serve at once. Green beans or peas go well.

Carp, Eel or Pike in Red Wine

5 lb. carp, eel or pike
20–30 small onions
1 lb. carrots, cubed
10 cloves garlic
½ lb. streaky bacon, cubed
1 bottle red wine

In this recipe the whole fish is required. Also a suitably large oven dish. Cooking times obviously depend on the size of fish, but I am working here on 1 hour for a 5 lb. carp.

Clean and gut your fish, leaving the head on. Soak the fish in frequently changed, fresh cold water for 4 or 5 hours.

Fry the bacon for a few moments along with the carrots, onion and the cloves of garlic. When they are beginning to soften, place the fish on top and cover the lot with the red wine. Cover with tin foil. Bake in oven at 180°C/350°F/gas 4 for about 1 hour.

When the fish is cooked, remove and keep hot. Transfer the juices to the top of the stove and reduce by about ⅓. Pour over the fish.

Serve with lots of fresh bread and more wine.

Cod Cutlets with Aioli
Serves 6

6 × 4 oz. cod cutlets
juice 1 lemon
6 stoned black olives
4 oz. butter
seasoned flour
aioli – page 8
salt and pepper
chopped parsley

Season the cod cutlets with lemon juice and salt and pepper. Pass through the seasoned flour and knock off excess.

Melt the butter in a pan and fry the cutlets for about 4 minutes on each side.

Place on a serving dish and cover each cutlet with the aioli. Garnish with a black olive and some chopped parsley. Serve with boiled potatoes.

Drink a chilled red wine.

Monkfish with Paprika Sauce
Serves 6

6 thick fillets monkfish
6 rindless streaky bacon rashers
juice 1 lemon
2 glasses dry white wine
½ pint double cream
pinch thyme and rosemary – sprigs would be better

chopped parsley
2 oz. butter
paprika
tomato purée

Season the fish and dredge in paprika. Wrap each fillet in a rasher of bacon.

Place the fish in an oven dish with the butter. Squeeze the lemon juice over and sprinkle herbs on. Bake in a hot oven until the bacon is nearly cooked. Add the white wine and stir well into the fat from the bacon and the juices from the fish. Cook for 8 minutes more.

Remove the fish from the oven and place on a serving dish to keep warm. Add the cream and tomato purée to the juices in the dish and bubble on a low flame until all have amalgamated.

Strain the sauce over the fish and decorate with the chopped parsley.

Monkfish Roasted with Bacon and Garlic
Serves 6

6 thick fillets monkfish
6 rindless streaky bacon rashers
18 cloves peeled garlic – yes 18
juice 1 lemon
2 glasses dry white wine
½ pint double cream
pinch thyme and rosemary – sprigs would be better
2 oz. butter
chopped parsley
salt and pepper

To prevent your monkfish from going rubbery, remember to take the thin film off the fish – it will make the world of difference.

Season the fish and wrap each fillet in a rasher of bacon.

Place the fish and the peeled garlic in an oven dish with the butter. Squeeze the lemon juice over and sprinkle the herbs on.

Bake in a hot oven until the bacon is nearly cooked – about 10 minutes and the fish is almost ready too.

Add the white wine and stir well into the fat from the bacon and the juice from the fish. Cook for 8 minutes more.

Remove from oven and place fish on a serving dish and keep warm. Add the cream to the juices in the dish and bubble over a low flame until all have amalgamated.

Arrange the garlic around the fish and strain the sauce over them. Decorate with chopped parsley. Plain boiled rice is great and a chilled light red wine will wash it down well. And tell your guests not to worry about eating the garlic, it really won't be as strong as they imagine.

Monkfish with Cream and Brandy
Serves 4

1½ lb. monkfish, cut in ½" thick discs
seasoned flour
1 measure brandy
1 teaspoon mild mustard
6 oz. double cream
juice 1 lemon
4 oz. finely sliced mushrooms
1 finely chopped shallot
1 oz. finely grated gruyère or other hard cheese
2 oz. butter
chopped parsley

Fry shallot and mushrooms in butter.

Squeeze the lemon over the fish and pass through the seasoned flour. Add the fish to the pan and fry briskly until the fish starts to get golden. Add the brandy and flame it using the cream to extinguish the flames. Remove the fish and keep warm.

Meanwhile stir in the mustard and the grated cheese until the cheese melts. Then mask the fish with the sauce and place under a hot grill until it turns golden.

Fried potatoes, a green salad and a strong white wine would be in order here.

Grey Mullet with Mustard
Serves 4

1 whole grey mullet, descaled and gutted with head left on
2 tablespoons good but mild French mustard
3 oz. butter
parsley, finely chopped
1 large onion, cut in fine rings
1 glass white wine
pinch herbes de Provence (mixed herbs)
salt and pepper
juice 1 lemon

Wipe the fish dry and check that it is clean and dry inside.

Cut 4 incisions ¼" deep on each side of the fish. Season well with salt and pepper, lemon juice and the herbes de Provence.

Put the butter in each of the incisions and place on a bed of the onion rings in a grilling tray. Cook for 10 minutes each side under a very hot grill.

Now fill the incisions with the mustard and pour the wine into the pan. Return to the grill for a further 10 minutes until the skin is crisp and the mustard has flowed over the fish and mixed with the butter and juices forming an unctuous and piquant sauce. Garnish with parsley and serve.

Scallops with Cointreau on a Skewer
Serves 4

16 large scallops
16 thin rashers streaky bacon – with the rind off
1 or 2 teaspoons oregano
juice 1 lemon
large measure Cointreau
6 tablespoons double cream
2 oz. butter
salt and black pepper
chopped fresh parsley

Turn on the grill to maximum heat.

Wrap each scallop in bacon and thread onto skewers. Place the four skewers on a tray and season with lemon juice, butter, salt, pepper and oregano.

Put under the grill and as the bacon cooks, turn the skewers round. When the bacon is cooked so too will be the scallops.

Remove your tray with the scallops to a low heat on the stove. Pour over the Cointreau and flame. Extinguish the flames with the cream and stir the juices from the tray, the Cointreau and the cream together. Bubble for a moment or two to allow to thicken.

Serve the scallops on the skewers with the sauce poured over. Garnish with parsley. Simple boiled rice goes well.

Scallops with Pernod on a Skewer
Serves 4

16 large fresh scallops – frozen will do if defrosted gently
16 thin rashers smoked streaky bacon – with the rind off
2 tablespoons double cream
½ measure Pernod
1 teaspoon oregano
juice 2 lemons
3 oz. butter
chopped fresh parsley or chives

Wrap each scallop in a rasher of bacon and thread onto 4 skewers. Season with oregano, salt and pepper. Put the skewers on a tray with the butter and set under hottest grill, turning as the bacon cooks. Watch that the juice coming from the scallops does not evaporate. Continue cooking for about 10 minutes – the scallops should be just undercooked.

Put the tray and the scallops on a low gas and pour over the Pernod. Flame it and extinguish at once with the lemon juice. Remove the scallops onto a serving dish. Add the cream to the juices in the tray, bubble for a second or two and pour over each skewer. Garnish with chopped parsley. Spoil yourself with some mange tout peas and a bottle of good white Burgundy.

Baked Trout with Hollandaise Sauce
Serves 4

1 Trout, at least 2 lbs. in weight – cleaned and gutted
juice 1 lemon
leeks, cut into fine strips
onions, cut into fine strips
carrots, cut into fine strips
2 glasses dry white wine
salt and pepper
hollandaise sauce – page 9
good supply lemon wedges

When cleaning and gutting the fish remember to scrape out the black tube which runs along the spine.

Liberally salt and pepper the inside of the fish and rub with the juice of a lemon.

Butter an oven tray and lay the fish on a bed of the leeks, onions and carrots which you have cut into very fine julienne strips. Pour over the white wine, cover with tin foil and bake for about 10 minutes per pound at 190°C/375°F/gas 5.

Serve on a large white dish with the vegetables strewn over the trout and surrounded by small boiled new potatoes. Serve the hollandaise sauce in a jug. Simple and delicious.

A good supply of lemon wedges on another dish – soggy lemon pieces floating in the sauce are not wanted – is recommended.

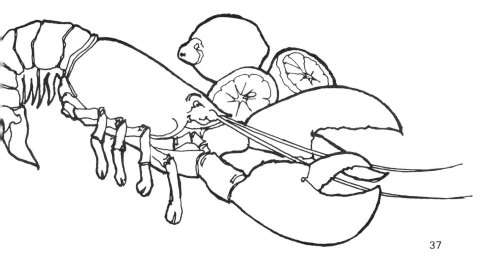

Salmon Escalopes with Watercress
Serves 6

slices of fresh salmon as required
1 glass fish stock – optional
2 bunches watercress, finely chopped
1 shallot or chives, finely chopped
juice 1 lemon
8 oz. double cream
grated nutmeg
salt and pepper
3 glasses dry white wine
2 oz. unsalted butter

Marinate the salmon slices in the lemon juice, seasoned with salt and pepper, for 15 minutes.

Melt the butter in a pan large enough to hold the salmon and fry the shallot until soft but not brown. Add the white wine, turn up the heat and allow to boil for a few moments (this burns off unwanted alcohol and leaves the flavour). Reduce gas, add the fish and poach very gently for 3 or 4 minutes – if the fish is not covered by the wine add a glass of water, or fish stock if you are highly organised. Remove the cooked fish very carefully and place on a serving dish.

Add the very finely chopped watercress to the juices in the pan and cook for a further 2 minutes. Add fresh cream, season with nutmeg, stirring all the time over a low heat so as to avoid curdling the cream. When the sauce has reached the consistency of thinnish custard pour over the salmon and serve with an accompaniment of new carrots.

Main Dishes

The Grilling Factor
Chicken Breast with Langoustines
Chicken with Cream and Butter
Chicken with Rosemary and Tomato Sauce
Coq au Vin, as it should be
Duck with Green Peas
Quail
To Roast a Young Grouse
To Cook Old Grouse
Guinea Fowl with Peaches
Gourmet's Roast Pheasant, without the hanging saga
Beef in Red Wine
Floyd's Goulasch
Oxtail with Grapes
Pork with Apple and Calvados
Roast Pork Provençale
Lamb Kebab with Yoghurt Sauce
Neck of Lamb Sauté
Roast Lamb with Vegetables
Calves' Liver with Mustard Sauce
Calves' Sweetbreads
Lamb's Kidneys with Grapes
Venison with Crème de Cassis Sauce

All the dishes in this section, as with all the recipes in the book, are cooked or have been cooked by me in my restaurants over the years. Some I have trimmed so that they can become a more realistic proposition for the domestic cook, whilst ensuring that none of the flavours are impaired.

Here are just a few quick points to help in our pursuit of successful cooking:

wine in cooking – if it is not good enough to drink it is not good enough to cook with. Always preboil the wine before use, this will get rid of any unpleasant alcoholic tastes.

roasting – always try to remember to save any unused fat or stock from the roasting pan. A fine jelly resulting from a roasted joint is invaluable for making the sauce for 'venison with crème de cassis' or for enrichening the sauce for the 'kidneys with grapes'.

casseroles – always seal the meat before cooking and always cook very slowly, with barely a movement in the liquid. If when the meat is cooked and you find the sauce too thin, remove the meat and any vegetables and reduce by simmering on the stove. If there is too little sauce, preboiled wine or vegetable water or perhaps some of the all important roasting jelly can be added. Remember, casseroles always improve quite strikingly with keeping – when cold, the fat that settles on top can easily be removed.

The Grilling Factor

Here is what I hope will be a very useful section on how to produce perfect grilled meats. The irony is that in order to attain perfection you must NOT use the grill, as domestic ones are seldom hot enough to 'grill' meat successfully. Instead, very fast and very hot frying in a heavy metal pan is the secret.

You will need:

1. A heavy metal frying pan – or chargrill/barbecue if you own one
2. Herbs, fresh if possible
      lamb – rosemary
      veal – sage
      steak – garlic
      pork – thyme
3. Butter
4. Salt and black pepper
5. Sauce of your choice
      tomato – page 12
      Onion – page 13
      béarnaise – page 10
      mustard – page 9
6. Cooking times
      steak – approximately 2 minutes or less each side
      veal – approximately 3 minutes or less each side
      lamb – approximately 4 minutes or less each side
      pork – approximately 5 minutes or less each side

The steak, veal and lamb should all be beautifully pink. The pork, whilst not pink, should certainly be juicy and succulent not dried out and dreary.

Method

Heat your pan absolutely dry and very hot and stand poised with the herbs, salt and black pepper. Seal your meat quickly on both sides and season. Press the meat into the pan until smoke gets in your eyes and cook for appropriate time – turn over and repeat.

Serve on a hot plate with a knob of butter, the chips your husband has made and the salad your children have expertly thrown together.

Chicken Breast with Langoustines
Serves 4

4 small chicken breasts
4 langoustines per person – fresh water crayfish or whole
 king prawns can be used
1 tablespoon finely chopped onion
1 clove garlic, chopped
1 tablespoon parsley, chopped
1 coffee cup of tomato sauce – page 12
1 coffee cup double cream
2 oz. butter
1 large glass white wine
1 measure Cognac
pinch thyme
salt and pepper
1 tablespoon jellified chicken gravy – if available
1 teaspoon dry sherry – if required

Season the chicken and fry gently in butter for 10 minutes or so, until almost cooked.

Add the onions, garlic, thyme and langoustines – if necessary throw in a little more butter. Flame with the Cognac and add the white wine. Allow to simmer for a few moments.

Add the tomato sauce and the cream and if possible a tablespoon or two of jellified gravy left over from a previous roast. Taste the sauce, it should not be too creamy. Season with salt and pepper. At this stage a teaspoon of sherry could be added to sharpen the sauce up a little. Serve with plainly boiled rice and a green salad.

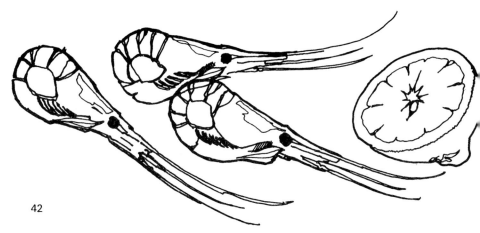

Chicken with Cream and Butter

Serves 4

1 chicken – marinated in lemon juice, thyme, salt and
  pepper for 5 hours
½ lb. butter
2 egg yolks, beaten
small tub double cream

Roast your chicken, breast down in the butter, at 180°C/350°F
gas 4 basting all the while. After 30 minutes turn the bird breast
up, the gas up to 5 and finish cooking turning the bird golden.
Place chicken on serving dish and keep warm.

Take the roasting tray with all its juices and put on a low gas.
Gently stir in the cream, taking care to mix it well with even those
little bits stuck to the tray.

Reduce the heat to an absolute minimum and stir in the 2 beaten
egg yolks quickly to the sauce which will now thicken. Remove
from heat at once and strain over the chicken. Serve immediately
with a fruity light red wine.

Chicken with Rosemary and Tomato Sauce

Serves 4

1 chicken jointed into 8 pieces
oil – enough to cover the chicken in a high sided pan
1 heaped tablespoon rosemary spikes – not powder
juice 1 lemon
little flour
salt and pepper
2 cloves chopped garlic
½ pint tomato sauce – page 12

Smother the chicken pieces in garlic and plenty of black pepper, a
little salt and lemon juice for 1 hour before you cook.

Pre heat the fat – drop a cube of bread into it, if it turns golden
the fat is hot enough. Dust the chicken pieces in flour and deep
fry them – 10 minutes should be fine. Then add to the fat and the

chicken all the rosemary and continue cooking till chicken is crisp on the outside. Regulate the heat so that the spikes of rosemary do not burn.

Serve very hot and oil free. The chicken should be coated with rosemary and not at all oily. Accompany with tomato sauce and eat with your fingers.

Coq au Vin (as it should be)
Serves 6

1 5/6 lb. boiling fowl jointed into 12 pieces – don't throw away giblets
1 large onion, diced
½ lb. fatty bacon cut into ¼" cubes
2 cloves chopped garlic
sprig thyme
1 bay leaf
1 glass brandy
1 bottle red wine
4 oz. button mushrooms
flour
2 oz. butter
3 teaspoons sugar
salt and pepper

Dust the chicken pieces with flour and brown in butter along with bacon, onion and chopped garlic. Season well with salt and pepper.

Pour in the brandy and flame it. Cover the chicken pieces with red wine, add the herbs and giblets and cook slowly for 1 hour.

Just before serving, fry the mushrooms in butter and add to the coq au vin. Finally, add the sugar.

N.B. There should not be a lot of sauce, so it is a good idea to remove the chicken once cooked and to reduce the sauce by boiling rapidly for 10 minutes or so. This reduction will give a stronger flavour to the sauce.

Duck with Green Peas
Serves 4

1 oven ready fresh duck
1 lb. fresh garden peas, shelled
¼ lb. diced bacon
2 cloves chopped garlic
1 onion, finely diced
4 oz. diced carrots
butter
pinch sage or a leaf or two
2 glasses white wine
cup water
salt and pepper

Melt some butter in a roasting pan. Brown the duck on all sides along with the onions, bacon, carrots and garlic.

Then roast breast down at 180°C/350°F/gas 4 for 20 minutes. Turn the duck breast up, add the peas, wine, water and sage and season with salt and pepper. Finish cooking until the duck is crisp and the peas tender.

Joint the duck and surround with the peas and juices from the pan. The bird is now beautifully ready to eat.

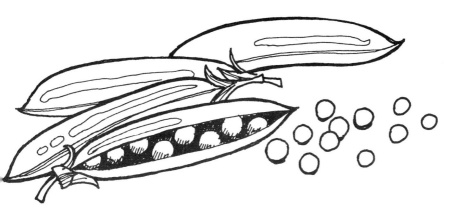

Quail

2 quail per person
1 crouton trimmed to fit each bird
8 cloves garlic per person – unpeeled
twigs fresh thyme and rosemary
olive oil
tin of anchovy fillets
1 rasher bacon per bird
measure brandy, eau de vie or Armagnac
salt and pepper

Stuff each quail with a twig of rosemary and thyme. Season with salt and pepper and wrap in one rasher of bacon. On each crouton put one or two anchovy fillets and put the quail on top.

Lightly oil a grilling tray. Put on the quail surrounded by the garlic still in its skin. Sprinkle the lot with olive oil and place under a hot grill for about 15 minutes, turning the birds from time to time to ensure that they cook evenly.

When cooked flame the lot with your alcohol and serve at once with a salad of dandelion leaves (page 71). Remember to reassure your guests that the garlic cloves will taste very much like roasted chestnuts. They may then have the courage to eat them!

To Roast a Young Grouse

1 grouse per person
pinch thyme per bird
butter
1 crouton per bird
salt and pepper

Remove the liver from the bird. Place the liver on the crouton with a knob of butter.

Season the grouse with salt, pepper and a pinch of thyme and seal rapidly in hot butter in a frying pan on top of the stove.

Place the bird on the crouton and pop into a hot oven for 20 minutes, basting with lots of butter.

Whack the grouse onto a hot plate and strain all the butter from the roasting tray over it. Eat with watercress and little fried potatoes.

And should you have a bottle of Corton to hand the twelfth will be even more glorious.

To Cook Old Grouse
Serves 4

1 grouse per person
2 lb. cabbage leaves
3 rashers fatty bacon, diced
2 carrots, diced
1 onion, diced
1 bay leaf
4 crushed juniper berries
6 oz. sausage meat – seasoned with salt, pepper and 1
   teaspoon sage
1 bottle dry white wine
2 oz. butter
black pepper

Blanch the cabbage leaves in boiling water for 5 minutes. Strain them and leave to cool.

In a heavy casserole melt the butter and fry the onions, carrots and bacon until soft but not coloured (or golden as we say in the trade). Add the birds briefly to the casserole to seal them.

Remove birds and stuff with the seasoned sausage meat. Then wrap each bird in several leaves of cabbage and return to casserole.

Cover with white wine, add juniper berries and the bay leaf. Throw in another knob of butter, give a good few twists of the black pepper mill, put on the lid and pop into the oven on a low heat for 1 hour or so.

And this in the parlance of cook books will make a substantial lunch for a cold day and a warm bottle of your best red wine.

Guinea Fowl with Peaches
Serves 4

1 large guinea fowl, about 2 lbs.
4 fresh ripe peaches, halved
3 oz. butter
salt, pepper, thyme and basil
juice 1 lemon
measure brandy or peach liqueur
1 glass white wine
(if you have saved the fat from your last roasted fowl there
    will be some jelly underneath it which will come in handy)

*This fabulous dish is very nearly as delicious when spring
chickens (poussin) are used.*

Season the bird inside and out with the salt, pepper, thyme and
basil. Rub with lemon juice and butter and place in a hot oven
for 15 minutes, breast down.

Then add the peaches and the wine and cook for a further 15
minutes breast up, basting frequently. When the skin is brown
and the flesh moist (it must not be overcooked) remove the bird
and joint it. Place with the peaches onto a serving dish, pour over
the brandy and ignite.

Meanwhile bubble the juices in the roasting pan until the volume
is reduced by half. Then add the jelly (which you have sensibly
saved from your previous roast) and the juices which have oozed
from the flamed bird on the serving dish. There is not much sauce
but it is delicious so don't cook it away. Strain over the guinea
fowl and serve at once.

Gourmet's Roast Pheasant (without the hanging saga)

Serves 4

1 plump unhung pheasant (*rotting flesh and thick red floury sauces with stuffing and jam are positively out*)
4/5 oz. butter
salt, pepper and thyme
2 glasses red wine

Season your bird with salt, pepper and thyme and fry in the butter until golden on all sides – don't burn the butter or the pheasant. Then place breast down on an oven dish with the butter and roast for 15 minutes at gas 5 on the left breast and then for a further 15 minutes on the right breast. This system, as for the guinea fowl recipe, allows the breasts to stay moist while the tougher legs cook through. Baste frequently! Add more butter if necessary for the more you baste the better the result.

Now place the bird upright and add the wine and cook for a further 15 minutes. Jab a fork in a leg to check that it is cooked and remove from pan and carve, saving carefully any juices to add to the sauce in the roasting dish.

You must now bubble the sauce, with the juices added, on top of the stove for 2 or 3 minutes. Taste, season with pepper and if necessary add a knob of butter. Pour this thin sauce over the pheasant and serve with matchstick chips or other fried potatoes.

Beef in Red Wine
Serves 6

2/2½ lb. stewing beef, cut into 2" or 3" pieces
½ lb. fatty bacon, cut into ¼" cubes
4 cloves garlic, crushed
15 to 18 very small onions
1 lb. carrots, cut in half to make fingers
½ lb. small mushrooms
1 bottle strong red wine
fresh parsley, chopped
sprig thyme
salt and pepper
a little flour
fat for frying meat
1 bayleaf

This dish, generally called boeuf bourguignonne, is one frequently and ritually murdered in many small restaurants all over the country – which is a great shame as it is a marvellously simple and successful dish to cook. Follow this straightforward recipe and you will be amazed that you've been paying good money for it!

Dip the meat lightly in flour and shake off excess. Season with salt and pepper and fry till brown along with the garlic and bacon.

Put the meat into a good casserole with a lid.

In the residue of the fat in the frying pan, fry the vegetables for a few minutes. Add them to the beef in the casserole, cover with the wine, pop in the herbs and drop on the lid. Cook very slowly in the oven or on top for about 2 hours or until the meat is tender. At no time must the dish boil – not even to begin with – for if it cooks very slowly with just the slightest bubble breaking the surface the resulting sauce will be meaty, winey and supreme.

Floyd's Goulasch
Serves 6

2/2½ lb. diced stewing beef
4 cloves chopped garlic
½ lb. onion slices
3 oz. paprika – yes 3 oz!
1 bayleaf
pinch of thyme
salt and pepper
oil for frying meat
teaspoon caraway seeds
14 oz. tin tomatoes and their juice
1 tablespoon tomato purée
1 teaspoon cayenne powder
½ pint soured cream
chopped parsley to garnish

I once sold a restaurant to a chef who had worked for me. His idea for my goulasch was to add paprika and tomato purée to my 'beef in red wine' recipe – he said no one would be able to tell the difference. This is how it should be done!

Dredge the meat lightly in flour. Shake off excess and smother in paprika. Season with salt and pepper and fry with chopped garlic until brown. When browned put meat into a heavy casserole.

In the fat from the meat fry the onions until brown and add to the casserole. Put all except the parsley and soured cream into casserole and add 1 full cup of water. Cook covered very slowly in oven or on top for about 2 hours or until meat is tender. Serve garnished with soured cream and parsley. Accompany with rice. This excellent dish should be red and pink with little balls of yellow oil floating on top.

And to drink? Why not a good cold lager with vodka or schnapps chasers.

Oxtail with Grapes
Serves 6

1 large jointed oxtail
1 lb. depipped grapes – a can will do
1 large glass sherry
1 bayleaf
teaspoon thyme
large onion, diced
2 large carrots, finely diced
1 clove chopped garlic
1 tablespoon chopped parsley
1 tablespoon tomato purée
salt and pepper

This dish should be cooked the day before.

Trim excess fat off the oxtail.

In a heavy pan brown the meat with the onions, carrots and garlic. Strain off excess fat and then flame in the sherry.

Stir in the tomato purée, add the herbs, season with salt and pepper and cover with water and cook very slowly with the lid on for at least 2 hours.

When cooked remove from the stove and allow to cool. Skim off fat from the surface.

To serve, add the grapes and reheat gently until the fruit is tender. Accompany with purée of potatoes – page 81.

Pork with Apple and Calvados
Serves 4

4 best end chops, well trimmed with no rind and little fat
4 oz. apple purée
¼ pint double cream
1 oz. butter
measure calvados
1 tablespoon meat jelly, which you have saved from your
  roasts
pinch sage
pinch nutmeg
salt and pepper

Season the chops with the sage and nutmeg. In a hot frying pan melt the butter and cook the chops gently, turning once for about 10 minutes (longer of course if the chops are a foot thick).

There should be some juice in the pan by now, so add the calvados and flame it. Remove the meat, pour in the apple purée, and cream and bubble until thick. Then add your meat jelly to thin the sauce a little, check the seasoning and pour over the chops. Eat at once.

Roast Pork Provençale
Serves 6-8

2 lb. boned and rolled loin pork – with rind off but with
  plenty of fat
2 lb. tinned tomatoes and the juice – they are better for
  cooking than insipid fresh ones grown under plastic
2 lb. white dried haricot beans – which you have soaked
  overnight
1 onion, finely chopped
8 cloves garlic, chopped
1 tablespoon parsley, finely chopped
1 bottle dry white wine

sprig thyme
sprig rosemary
1 bayleaf
salt and pepper

*This dish is France's answer to America's pork 'n' beans as eaten
by the cowboys.*
Simply whack the lot into an earthenware roasting dish, cover
with tinfoil and cook 180°C/350°F/gas 4 for about 2 hours. Add a
cup of water if the beans look like drying up. You won't need other
vegetables.
Couldn't be easier, could it?

Lamb Kebab and Yoghurt Sauce

1 leg lamb, cut into cubes

For the marinade:
10 coriander corns, crushed
1 cup olive oil
1 tablespoon turmeric
1 cup yoghurt
1 teaspoon salt
juice 2 lemons
1 tablespoon Tandoori powder

For the sauce:
1 or 2 teaspoons concentrated mint sauce per tub of yoghurt

*This is an excellent barbecue party dish where the guests do all
the cooking. All you do is buy the leg of lamb, cube it, marinate
and thread onto skewers. The yoghurt sauce is the work of a
moment.*
Mix all the marinade ingredients together. Leave the meat in the
marinade for at least 2 hours but all day if you can.

Neck of Lamb Sauté
Serves 6

6 meaty neck cutlets
½ lb. fresh carrots
1 lb. broad beans
1 lb. new potatoes
3 fresh tomatoes cut in half
1 lb. fresh garden peas
6 artichoke hearts – discard the leaves
6 small peeled onions
1 pint milk
big sprig fresh mint
butter
fresh parsley, chopped
salt and pepper

This dish relies on the quality of the vegetables used rather than the meat – of which there will not be much. It is therefore very important that you do not attempt this dish without fresh ingredients.

Fry the meat gently in butter for 15 minutes. Put to one side.

In the same butter fry gently the onions and carrots until soft – not cooked. Put them in a heavy pan on the stove with the potatoes. Cover with milk and season. Cook very slowly for about 30 minutes. Then add all of the other ingredients and cook until tender. Serve with knobs of melting butter on each plate.

Iced fizzy pink wine by the bucketful is required.

Roast Lamb with Vegetables
Serves 4-6

1 leg lamb
12 small 1" onions
6 very small turnips
6 medium sized potatoes
12 pieces carrot
12 cloves unpeeled garlic
1 branch rosemary
½ bottle white wine
salt and pepper

Season the lamb well with salt and pepper and stud it with half the garlic.

Cut all the vegetables to a uniform size, taking the onions as a guide.

In a roasting pan brown the vegetables slightly and place the meat on top of them with the rosemary and the rest of the garlic. Roast in a medium oven for 40 minutes, checking from time to time that the vegetables are cooking evenly.

Add the wine and turn up the oven to brown the meat and glaze the vegetables, for another 15 minutes or so. You should baste the meat with the wine at least twice during this period.

Leaving the vegetables in the oven, remove the meat to a carving pan which has guttering to catch the juices. Carve the meat and put onto a hot serving dish. Surround with the vegetables and the juices from the pan and the carving pan.

The lamb like your wine today should be pink.

Calves' Liver with Mustard Sauce
Serves 4

4 thin slices liver
1 measure Armagnac
1 tablespoon mild French mustard
4 tablespoons double cream
butter
flour
salt and pepper
chopped parsley

Sprinkle the liver lightly with flour and season with salt and pepper.

Melt the butter in a frying pan and fry the liver quickly for about 2 minutes on each side. Pour over the Armagnac and flame it. Remove the liver and keep hot.

Add the mustard and cream to the juices in the pan and bubble for a moment. If any juice has seeped from the liver add this to the sauce in the pan before pouring over the liver. Sprinkle with the chopped parsley.

Serve at once and hot, ignoring any protestations that the liver is pink. Sit back and sip your wine – a Brouilly or Mercurey perhaps?

Calves' Sweetbreads
Serves 4

1½ lb. calves' sweetbreads – if unavailable use lambs'
4 oz. butter
pinch nutmeg
4 lemon halves
1 tablespoon capers
1 tablespoon finely chopped parsley
flour
salt and pepper

Clean your sweetbreads under cold running water for about 2 hours, depending on how much blood there is to get rid of.

Then sometime before you intend to eat them blanch them in boiling salted water, allow to cool, peel off the fine outer skin (get someone else to do it for you, it's a bore) and press them between two plates with weights on for an hour – if they are large, slice them into scallops of 2" in diameter.

Dry them carefully, season, sprinkle with flour and fry gently in half the butter until they become absolutely golden. The pan will now be thick with little bits of burnt butter and flour so take out the sweetbreads, get a new pan and gently melt the rest of the butter till it foams and turns brown.

Pop the sweetbreads back in with the capers, parsley and pinch of nutmeg and swish them quickly around the pan. Serve at once on hot plates with your lemon halves and another bottle of rosé from the case which you bought for the kidneys.

Lamb's Kidneys with Grapes
Serves 4

8 lamb's kidneys
1 glass dry sherry
½ lb. depipped grapes
1 tablespoon very finely chopped onion
2 oz. butter for frying
flour
milk
salt and pepper

This simple dish is quite delicious if you obey the rules:

Rule 1 – remove the fine outer skin from the kidney
Rule 2 – cut the kidneys in half and remove fatty gristle from inside
Rule 3 – don't overcook the little dreams, they should be faintly
pink
Rule 4 – marinate then in milk for 2 hours before cooking. This
removes any nasty tastes.

Having thus obeyed, you season the kidneys, sprinkle with flour
and fry briskly in butter for 3 or 4 minutes, turning often. Add the
sherry and flame it till the juices run from the kidneys. Then whip
in the grapes and bubble till they are cooked – don't let the liquid
evaporate.

Serve at once with some sauté potatoes and a crisp, very cold
rosé and you will see that kidneys rule . . . O.K?

Venison with Crème de Cassis Sauce
Serves 4

4 × 5 oz. fillets venison – or the boned out saddle of a fawn
   cut into 4
1 measure crème de cassis
1 oz. butter
1 teaspoon herbes de Provence (mixed herbs)
4/5 tablespoons jelly saved from your roasts
salt and lots of black pepper

Season your meat with salt, herbs and lots of black pepper. Fry
gently in the butter for about 3 minutes each side.

Flame with the cassis. Add your jelly and allow to bubble for a few
moments. The meat should be rare and the sauce very rich.

Serve with ribbon noodles in a creamy cheese sauce – page 80.
And a crisp green salad.

Miscellany

Cous Cous, simplified the Floyd way
Ham and Lettuce with Cheese Sauce
My Favourite Meal
My Moussaka
My Mum's Faggots
Paella Without Tears
Pasta with Olive Oil and Basil
Rabbit with Prunes
Scrambled Eggs with Truffles and Chives

What follows is a collection of dishes great and small from here, there and everywhere. They have no link other than that they are unconnected and would not happily fit in any other section. They are all delicious.

Cous Cous (simplified the Floyd way)
Serves 6

1 lb. cous cous – cooked to instructions on packet
1 boiling fowl, jointed
2 tins chick peas
1 large onion, chopped
1 large tin tomatoes and the juices
1 tablespoon very hot paprika or cayenne
3 courgettes, sliced
1 red pepper, chopped
1 aubergine, chopped
4 cloves chopped garlic
1 teaspoon turmeric
1 teaspoon thyme
2 bayleaves
oil for frying chicken
1 cup water
salt and pepper

Most health food shops sell cous cous these days and instructions for cooking it are on the packet. And joy of joys it has been treated so as to cook in about 4 minutes as opposed to the hours that the Arabs have to spend. Anyway, follow the packet instructions and you won't go far wrong.

Brown the chicken pieces in oil.

Season well with garlic, salt and pepper. Cover with all the other ingredients except for the cous cous and cook in a covered casserole on top of the stove on a low heat for about 1 hour.

When the chicken is tender, strain off all the sauce.

Mix all the bits, including the chicken, with the cous cous and reheat by steaming over boiling water in a colander – the cous cous must not touch the water or it will become mushy.

Serve at once with the reheated sauce poured over it.

And what about several litres of rough, strong, brown looking Algerian wine to go with this very, very spicy dish.

Ham and Lettuce with Cheese Sauce
Serves 4

8 slices cooked ham
hearts of 2 crisp lettuces, coarsely shredded and thoroughly
  dry
½ pint béchamel sauce – page 11
4 oz. grated gruyère type cheese
pinch nutmeg
pepper

Put half the lettuce in a shallow earthenware dish and cover with slices of ham. Then cover the ham with the remainder of the lettuce.

Make your béchamel sauce and mask the lettuce with it. Sprinkle over some black pepper and then the cheese and nutmeg. Bake in a hot oven for 15 minutes. Brown under the grill to finish off.

Eat with lots of fresh bread.

My favourite Meal
Serves 1

¼ loaf French bread sliced lengthways
6 raw onion rings
2 anchovy fillets
thin slices Cheddar cheese
tomato ketchup

Tomato ketchup has no function in the kitchen except as an ingredient in 'my favourite meal' – sorry Heinz.

Arrange the cheese, onions and anchovies on the bread and put under a hot grill until the cheese melts and the edges of the bread burns.

Dose liberally with tomato ketchup and munch away, smiling deprecatingly and saying 'well, cooking all day like I do, I don't feel like much at this time of night . . .'

My Moussaka
Serves 4

1 lb. minced cooked lamb – from Sunday's joint
1 large onion, finely chopped
14 oz. tin tomatoes
1 tablespoon chopped parsley
1 teaspoon thyme or rosemary
1 bayleaf
1 pint thick but not floury béchamel sauce – page 11
4 oz. grated cheese
1 large aubergine, sliced into thin discs
oil for frying
4 cloves chopped garlic
salt and pepper

Fry the aubergine discs in shallow oil until cooked – about 10 minutes.

Remove the aubergines and in the same oil fry the onions until golden. Add the meat, garlic, herbs and tin of tomatoes. Season to taste and cook for 10 minutes on a fast gas until there is not much liquid left.

Tip the meat mix into a shallow oven proof dish and cover with the aubergines. Mask with the béchamel sauce, sprinkle with cheese and bake in the oven until the top is golden.

Serve with boiled rice or pasta and drink some retsina and although this is no great gastronaut dish it should taste better than the Greek version you had on holiday.

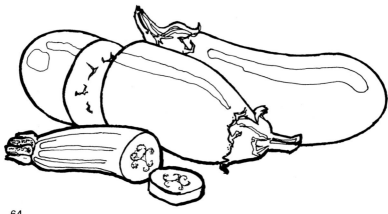

My Mum's Faggots

1 set pig's lights
2 lb. pig's liver
3 large onions, cut in half
1 tablespoon dried sage
1 tablespoon chopped parsley
salt and pepper
1 teaspoon thyme
1 bayleaf
2 leaves sage or 1 teaspoon dried
2 Oxo cubes – Keith's mum says nothing else will do (Ed.)
1 packet marrowfat dried peas according to recipe on box
  but add 1 tablespoon sugar

You ask the butcher for pig's lights and he will give you an unspeakable mess of intestines – make sure he gives you lots of 'caul', a sort of fat netting without which a faggot is not a faggot!

In a large saucepan put the lights, liver and onions and cover with water. Pop in the bayleaf, 2 teaspoons salt and the second lot of sage. Simmer for about 1 hour until the onions et al are cooked. (*Your average gastronaut will by now be moaning like hell about the smell – remind him about those 'caillettes' he wolfed down in that 'super little Routier' in Provence last year* – and peace will *return*).

Strain off the liquid into another saucepan. Put onto a low gas to reduce by about one third.

Take the offal and onions and mince it all coarsely, mixing in the sage, parsley, thyme, salt and pepper.

Form the mixture into balls a bit smaller than tennis balls and wrap each one with a generous section of caul. Place on a roasting dish and moisten liberally with some of the stock. Bake in the oven until the caul is cooked – about 10 minutes.

Meanwhile, add the Oxo cubes to the rest of the stock and thicken with just a little cornflour. Serve the faggots with marrowfat dried peas which you have turned mushy.

For nostalgic reasons I always eat mine in a white pudding basin; the kind with which I queued at the faggot van in the pouring rain of my childhood!

Paella without Tears
Serves 6

1 lb. 'quick cook' rice
1 small jointed chicken or rabbit
2 dozen mussels – frozen will do
¼ lb. peeled prawns
6 large prawns in their shells
1 teaspoon hot paprika or cayenne
1 tablespoon powdered turmeric – *even the Spanish seldom use saffron these days*
1 large onion, diced
4 cloves garlic, chopped
1 red pepper, finely diced
2 pints fish stock or water
olive oil for frying – 1 coffee cup at least
14 oz. tin tomatoes and their juice
salt and pepper

Season the chicken pieces in salt, pepper and paprika.

Then in a large frying pan gently fry the chicken, onions and garlic in some of the olive oil – until golden. Add more oil and stir in the uncooked rice, stirring until the oil is absorbed – about 5 minutes.

Now add everything else except the fish and cook gently until the rice is almost ready – roughly 20 minutes. Add the fish and turn up the heat to bubble away the liquid; another 10 minutes.

The rice is dry and fluffy, the chicken tender, the wine chilled and God is in his Spanish Heaven.

Pasta with Olive Oil and Basil
Serves 6

2 lb. spaghetti
¼ pint olive oil – at least
heaped saucer of freshly chopped basil leaves
grated Parmesan cheese
black pepper

If you are able, buy fresh spaghetti and use it for this superbly simple dish.

Cook your spaghetti 'al dente' in masses of salted boiling water. Strain and run under the hot tap to remove any starch or stickiness.

Meanwhile have ready a large mixing bowl into which you have put the basil and the olive oil. Add the spaghetti and mix thoroughly with at least 15 twists of your black pepper mill. Sprinkle to taste with Parmesan and eat at once with lashings of red wine.

'Spag. bol.' in the local trat. will never taste the same.

Rabbit with Prunes
Serves 4

1 jointed rabbit, about 2 lb.
¼ lb. smoked bacon, diced
½ lb. soaked prunes
1 heaped teaspoon strong mustard
20 very small onions
½ pint dry white wine
2 oz. butter
measure brandy
salt and pepper

Season the jointed rabbit and brown in butter. Put to one side.
Into the same butter brown the onions and bacon and put to one side.

Spread the mustard over the meat pieces and put the rabbit, onions, bacon and thyme into a casserole and cover with the wine. Cook for about 1 hour at 180°C/350°F/gas 4.

After 1 hour add the prunes and the brandy and cook for a further 30 minutes.

Scrambled Eggs with Truffles and Chives
Serves 4

8 large eggs
½ cup milk
3 oz. butter
2 tablespoons fresh double cream
1 chopped truffle – *alright, it costs £4 but the eggs are cheap*
2 tablespoons chopped fresh chives
salt and pepper
8 rounds toasted French bread

In a saucepan melt the butter. Add the chopped truffle and allow to cook for a minute. Add the eggs and milk in the normal way, whisking all the while. As the eggs set add the chives, cream and season with salt and pepper.

Serve on hot toast and garnish with a bit of our tomato sauce, if any is to hand.

Summer Suppers and Salads

Best Salad Dressing

Elaborate French Dressing

Cheese and Basil Salad

Dandelion Salad

Leftover Cooked Rice Salad

Salade Niçoise

Tomato Salad

Courgettes au Gratin

Creamed Carrots

Fresh Broad Beans and Bacon

Spinach Gateau

Stuffed Tomatoes

A collection of recipes for those few days in a calendar year that can truly be called summer.

The first half of the section concentrates on dressings and salads. The second on simple summer suppers based around the vegetables from your garden. All very light, very delicious and very simple.

Best Salad Dressing
Serves 4

1 lettuce, crisp and absolutely dry
1 clove garlic
2 teaspoons sherry vinegar
2 tablespoons olive oil

Having ensured that your lettuce is crisp and dry, you crush your clove of garlic into a salad bowl. Add the sherry vinegar and the olive oil. Put the lettuce on top and sprinkle with salt.

When ready to eat, toss the salad gently and patiently until all the leaves are coated – use your hands.

Elaborate French Dressing

1 cup olive oil
2 tablespoons wine vinegar
1 teaspoon mild French mustard
1 clove garlic, finely chopped
juice 1 large lemon
several twists of the pepper mill
2 teaspoons sugar

This is a French dressing for those of you who can't bear to leave out the kitchen sink.

Whisk the lot rapidly for a few moments. If it tastes too sharp, add a little more oil and sugar.

Cheese and Basil Salad
Serves 4

12 oz. cubed mozzarella cheese
2 tablespoons chopped fresh basil
1 clove chopped garlic
3 tablespoons olive oil

Mix all the ingredients together and eat with fresh bread but no butter – mop up the olive oil.

Dandelion Salad

Pick young, small, unflowering dandelion leaves. Wash and dry them carefully. Serve with olive oil, salt and sherry vinegar and cubes of hot fried bread.

Leftover Cooked Rice Salad

the leftover rice
14 oz. packet mixed nuts and raisins from your health store
pack of frozen peeled prawns
2 oz. pine nuts
chopped chives
some mayonnaise – page 9
1 finely chopped onion

Mix the lot together and you have Leftover Cooked Rice Salad.

I don't know how many it serves because it depends on the rice, does it not?

Salade Niçoise
Serves 6

6 hard boiled eggs, cut in half
12 or so cooked, cold green beans
12 black olives
6 sliced tomatoes
1 tin anchovy fillets
6 oz. tuna fish
head of crisp lettuce
few cubes left over boiled potatoes
salt and black pepper
1 wine glass olive oil
1 tablespoon sherry vinegar

Whack the lot into a salad bowl and eat it.

You may assure the querulous gastronaut that authentic salades niçioses do not have garlic in them. And one other thing, even in most Provençal restaurants it is worth demanding that they use olive oil.

Tomato Salad
Serves 4

1 lb. ripe tomatoes, finely sliced
1 tablespoon chopped fresh basil
½ teaspoon sugar
2 tablespoons olive oil
1 tablespoon sherry vinegar
1 teaspoon chopped fresh mint
salt and pepper

Cover the tomato slices with the mixed ingredients and leave to chill for 1 hour.

Courgettes au Gratin
Serves 4

2 lb. courgettes, cut into thin slices
1 lb. ripe tomatoes
4 oz. gruyère, grated
3 oz. Parmesan
1 oz. flour
3 tablespoons olive oil
oil for frying
1 teaspoon oregano
salt

Dust the courgette slices in flour and deep fry them until golden. Tip them onto kitchen paper and sprinkle them with salt to taste.

Liquidize the tomatoes.

Heat the oven to 220°C/425°F/gas 7.

Smear a soufflé dish or other oven proof pot with olive oil. Put in a layer of courgettes and then a layer of the puréed tomatoes and then a layer of grated gruyère. Repeat the layers until all ingredients are used. Sprinkle the oregano and the Parmesan over the top and pop in the oven for about 20 minutes.

Creamed carrots
Serves 4

2 lb. young carrots, washed and cut into $\frac{1}{4}$" batons
$\frac{1}{2}$ lb. diced cooked ham
heaped teaspoon fresh or dried tarragon
4 oz. butter
$\frac{1}{2}$ pint milk
2 teaspoons flour
black pepper

In the butter, fry the carrots and tarragon very gently until tender but not burnt – approximately 25 minutes.

Stir in the flour until smooth. Add the milk and cook until it thickens. Season with the black pepper and pour into a gratin dish. Strew the ham over the top and brown under the grill.

Fresh Broad Beans and Bacon
Serves 4

at least $\frac{1}{2}$ lb. bacon diced into 1 " pieces
2 lb. fresh broad beans from your garden – *which you were tending when the guests unexpectedly arrived*
finely grated cheese – a bowl of
dash olive oil
black pepper
1 clove chopped garlic

Blanch the beans for 3 minutes in boiling salted water.

Meanwhile heat your largest frying pan and add the olive oil, garlic, bacon and the strained beans. Mill over lots of black pepper and fry gently until the bacon is cooked and the beans are tender. Serve with the grated cheese.

Spinach Gateau
Serves 4

2 lb. spinach
2 soupspoons fresh cream
1 oz. butter

For the sauce:
14 oz. tin peeled tomatoes
1 carrot, very finely chopped
1 stick celery, very finely chopped
1 onion, very finely chopped
¼ lb. peas
1 oz. butter
tablespoon oil
salt and pepper

For the omelette:
4 eggs
¼ lb. grated gruyère
3 tablespoons fresh cream
salt, pepper and nutmeg

Cook the spinach without seasoning.

Meanwhile in a frying pan heat the oil and fry the carrot, onion and celery until golden. Then add the tomatoes (pulp them with a fork), the peas and some salt and cook gently for 15 minutes.

Strain the spinach and add the butter and fresh cream and cook for a further 10 minutes or until you have almost a thick purée. Put to one side.

Now is the time to make the omelettes. Add the cheese, cream, salt, pepper and nutmeg to the four eggs and make three omelettes.

Put one omelette into a round oven dish (a cake tin will do), cover with some spinach and some sauce and then another omelette which you cover as before. Carry on, finishing with spinach on top. Bake in a hot oven for 10 minutes.

Stuffed Tomatoes
Serves 4

8 large tomatoes, hollowed out with the pulp saved
4 oz. chicken livers
1 finely chopped onion
2 oz. prepared stuffing mix e.g. sage and onion
1 beaten egg
1 chopped clove garlic
8 stoned black olives
chopped fresh parsley or chives
olive oil
salt and pepper

Fry the livers in olive oil with the garlic and the onions. Allow to cool and then mash with a fork. Add the stuffing mix, tomato pulp and the egg and fill the tomatoes.

Season with salt and pepper, brush with olive oil and bake in a very hot oven for 15–20 minutes. Garnish with black olives and parsley.

And then all you need is bread and wine.

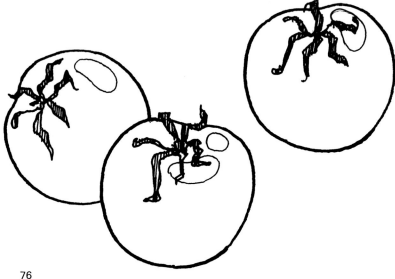

Vegetables

Chips

Matchstick Chips

Parsnip Chips

Carrots in White Wine

Deep Fried Courgettes or Aubergines

Deep Fried Cold Potatoes

Dried Beans

Fresh Garden Peas

Fresh Green Beans, Mange Tout,
Broad Beans etc.

Noodles in a Creamy Cheese Sauce

Potatoes Baked in Cream and Garlic

Purée Potatoes

Ratatouille

The rough rule for the cooking of vegetables is
that all those that grow above ground are
dropped gradually into already boiling water
whilst those that are grown under it are brought
to the boil.

Green vegetables, like beans, should be served
crisp. You can cook them well before, let them
cool and then when required gently reheat in
melted butter. I hope what follows will help you
to realise the best in your vegetables. They are as
important a part of the meal as the main dish.

Chips

Cut the potatoes into fine chips and then wash them several times in cold water. Dry them very carefully.

Cook in a medium hot fat until they are waxy – almost cooked but not brown. You can do this hours before you intend to use them, that way avoiding the panic while you are making the béarnaise and everybody else is getting sozzled in the garden.

At the time when you need them, heat the fat to super hot – use the bread test – and drop them in for just a few minutes until golden and wonderful.

Matchstick Chips

Rinse and dry as for ordinary chips but cook only once – at super heat until delicious.

Parsnip Chips

Parboil the parsnips, strain and dry. Cut into chips and deep fry. Absolutely delicious.

Carrots in White Wine

carrots, cut into slender batons
1 onion, finely chopped
lots of parsley, chopped
1 bayleaf
2 tablespoons sugar
1 large knob butter
white wine

In a pan put all the ingredients covering them with the white wine. Simmer until tender.

Deep Fried Courgettes or Aubergines

Cut your vegetables into very thin rounds. Soak in milk for 20 minutes or so.

Dredge in flour and fry until golden – just a few minutes. Strain the fat before using again!

Deep Fried Cold Potatoes

Cut your cold cooked potatoes into thin slices. Dip in flour and batter and deep fry. This is a very good kids' supper.

Dried Beans

Dried beans like haricot vert, haricot blanc and butter beans make smashing accompaniments to meals. And as cold left overs can make super hors d'oeuvres with a little oil and vinegar or tuna fish and imagination.

Follow the instructions on the packets. Don't forget to soak them in cold water for ages and always add a little fat or oil to the cooking liquid – better still throw in a pig's trotter or calf's foot or even a chicken carcass to add flavour along with a bayleaf, onion and carrot.

Fresh Garden Peas

your fresh garden peas
crisp lettuce, shredded
some cooked ham or streaky bacon, finely chopped
½ onion, finely chopped
1 tablespoon plain flour
stock cube
3 oz. butter
drop double cream

black pepper
few young carrots, finely chopped

*Except when picked very young garden peas are a disappointment.
And most gardeners are too mean to pick them young. So cook
them like this.*

Melt the butter in a pan with the bacon, onions and carrots and
fry for a moment or two. Add the lettuce – this will give off a
lot of liquid so stir in the flour until everything thickens. Add the
peas, the stock cube and a cup or two of water to thin out the
juice. Cook until the peas are really tender (this is longer than you
think).

Before serving twist the pepper mill generously over the dish, add
the cream and if you like another knob of butter.

Fresh Green Beans, Mange Tout, Broad Beans etc.

Drop them, little by little, into furiously boiling salted water for
minutes only. They should be slightly crisp, well strained and
served with butter and black pepper.

Noodles in a Creamy Cheese Sauce

Noodles – as required
equal quantities of béchamel sauce (Page 11) and single
 cream, mixed together
Parmesan cheese
black pepper

Cook the noodles in the usual way and strain them.

Return to the saucepan and cover with the béchamel sauce
equally mixed with the single cream. Stir in some grated Parmesan
cheese and reheat gently. Season well with black pepper.

Potatoes Baked in Cream and Garlic

thinly sliced raw potatoes
1 or 2 cloves garlic, crushed
salt, pepper and nutmeg
thick cream

Half fill a shallow earthenware dish with the sliced potatoes. Mix in your garlic, season well with the salt, pepper and nutmeg and cover with the cream (the potato should not be 'floating', hence the thick cream).

Bake in the oven 180°C/350°F/gas 4 for up to 1 hour depending on the quantity you make.

Purée Potatoes

2 lb. old potatoes
½ pint milk
4 oz. butter
2 eggs
pinch nutmeg
black pepper

Boil the potatoes in the normal way. Strain them and pass through a coarse sieve or mouli grater so that you have a pile of almost powdered pommes.

Heat the milk and melt the butter in it. Add the nutmeg and many twists of the pepper mill.

In a large bowl beat the eggs. Add the potatoes and whisking as for mayonnaise add the milk slowly. The result is only just short of a liquid and goes superbly well with grilled meat and other relatively sauce free dishes. If you are feeling frail, grate a little cheese into it and eat it on its own as a very nutritious supper.

Ratatouille
Serves 8-10

1 red pepper
1 green pepper
1 aubergine
1 courgette
2 onions
10 tomatoes
1 clove garlic, chopped
parsley, finely chopped
salt, pepper and thyme
most important of all, olive oil

*I hope this recipe will put those restaurants that serve some
ghastly mess of stewed vegetables under this name straight.*

The vitally important thing about ratatouille is that each vegetable
is cooked separately. So cut all the vegetables into equal sized
pieces – fork sized perhaps.

Prepare the aubergine and courgette first. Sprinkle them with salt
and leave them to 'sweat'. Then dry with kitchen paper.

In a large frying pan cook each vegetable in olive oil one after the
other until they are tender – put to one side with all the juices
from the pan. During this process, if necessary, top up the oil from
time to time. Now put the lot into a saucepan, add the garlic,
parsley, salt, pepper and thyme and all the left over oil and cook
for 10 or 15 minutes just to mix them all up. Leave to cool,
refrigerate and eat cold.

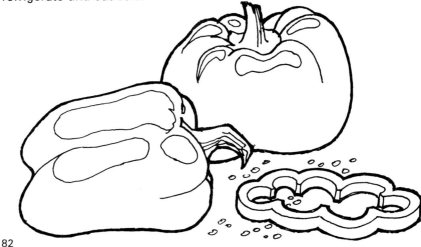

Sweets

Apple Tart

Friedbread Apple Pie

Fruit Idiot

Grilled Peaches

Melon with Muscat Beaumes
de Venise

Oranges in Caramel

Peach Pancakes

Pears in Red Wine

Pineapple Salad

The Strawberry Alternative

Beignets à la Confiture à la Façon de
ma Grand'mère
   or

Gastronaut Doughnuts

Stuffed Brandy Snaps

Chocolate Sauce for Ice Cream

Chocolate Mousse

Maureen's Chocolate Galette

Here is a collection of very simple and unusual
sweets. Only the fabulous Chocolate Galette
requires any great patience.

Apple Tart

Line a shallow sided 8" tart tin with sweet pastry (or use any kind of pastry if you are pushed).

Peel lots of apples and slice them into thin (and that means thin) crescent shapes and fill the pastry to the top. Sprinkle with sugar and bake at 200°C/400°F/gas 6 for 20 minutes or so.

Allow to cool and then melt some apricot jam and strain over the tart to glaze it.

Friedbread Apple Pie

sliced bread fingers – enough to cover a suitably sized pie
   dish twice over
apples, peeled, cored and sliced – to fill the pie dish
brown sugar – about 1 coffee cup full
lemon juice
cinnamon
butter
whipped cream

Fry the bread fingers in butter until crisp and golden.

Fry the apple slices in butter with the brown sugar, lemon juice and cinnamon until they are thick and sticky.

Cover the base of the pie dish with half the fried bread. Cover with the apple mixture. Now cover the apple with the rest of the fried bread. Sprinkle over lots more brown sugar and a few knobs of butter. Bake in a hot oven until crisp on top. Serve with lots of whipped cream.

It's amazingly good. When they ask you how you make the pastry just smile.

Fruit Idiot

Cook some soft fruit with sugar and no water for a few minutes. Then liquidize it so that you have a purée.

Whip up some cream until stiff. Mix the fruit and the cream together and pour into glasses. Refrigerate.

Grilled Peaches

Cut your peaches in half and remove the stone.

Fill the cavity with brown sugar, moisten with any alcohol handy and grill until the sugar caramelises. Serve at once with thick cream. And a glass of Beaumes de Venise.

Melon with Muscat de Beaumes de Venise

Nothing could be simpler. Just cut your melons in two, scoop out the pips and fill the resulting cavity with the wine. Chill and serve.

Oranges in Caramel
Serves 6

6 oranges, peeled, depipped and depithed
½ lb. caster sugar
Grandmarnier or a similar liqueur

Slice the oranges thinly and put into a heat proof bowl.

In a heavy bottomed pan put the caster sugar and set on a low gas, watching all the while as it melts and turns into a caramel colour. When it is quite liquid but not burnt pour over the oranges. Allow to cool and then splash over your Grandmarnier and serve.

Peach Pancakes

pancakes, as required
chopped peaches
butter to fry
dash orange squash
brandy
caster sugar

*The sensible gastronaut already has pancakes made up and
carefully frozen. So get them out of the freezer and defrost a few.*

Chop up some peaches and put a little on each pancake. Fold the
pancakes like envelopes or little parcels and set to fry gently in
melted butter. Add a dash of orange squash, turn up the heat and
as the liquid starts to reduce pour in some brandy and flame it.
Sprinkle in some caster sugar and serve at once.

*You can of course put any fruit you like inside the pancakes. It's
the principle that counts.*

Pears in Red Wine

pears – as many as there are people
red wine
cinnamon
2 tablespoons sugar per pear
1 lemon cut into slices

Peel the pears and pop into a saucepan. Cover with red wine and
stick in some cinnamon (a whole stick if you like), the lemon slices
and the sugar.

Bring to the boil and cook until soft. Remove the pears to a
decorative glass bowl. Continue cooking until the liquid is reduced
by one third. Pour over pears and allow to cool. They are better
the next day.

Pineapple Salad

1 large pineapple
1 large measure kirsch or other alcohol
1 heaped tablespoon caster sugar
1 small packet lemon sorbet or your own from the freezer

Cut off the top of the pineapple and save it.
Using your charm persuade someone to hollow out the fruit
without piercing the husk. Put half the sorbet at the bottom and
refill with the scooped out pineapple. Pour over the alcohol and
cover with the rest of the sorbet. Pop the lid back on and keep,
very, very cold until you need to eat it.

The Strawberry Alternative

Fill a glass bowl with strawberries. Cover liberally with caster
sugar, squeeze over the juice of two lemons and pour over half a
bottle of red wine. Leave in the fridge for several hours. Don't for
heaven's sake pour cream over them.

Beignets à la Confiture à la Façon de ma Grand'mère
or
Gastronaut Doughnuts

butterless jam sandwiches as required
fish batter
caster sugar

*A brilliant dessert when the cupboard is really bare and you dare
not admit that the deepfreeze is full of blackforest gateaux.*
Put the chip pan on the gas.
Cut the crusts off the sandwiches and slice into quarters. Dip in
the batter and fry till golden. Dredge liberally in the caster sugar
and serve. *You've just made the best doughnuts in town!*

Stuffed Brandy Snaps

brandy snaps, as required
1 pot ginger marmalade
small tub whipped cream

Mix the whipped cream with the ginger marmalade and pipe the resulting filling into the brandy snaps.
Tastes just great. They really do.

Chocolate Sauce for Ice Cream
Serves 6

½ lb. block of most expensive dark chocolate
1 measure brandy
1 teaspoon orange juice
½ oz. butter
1 tablespoon red wine

This superb sauce will revitalise even the most lack lustre of ice creams.
All you do is melt the lot together in a bain marie and serve.

Chocolate Mousse

½ lb. block expensive dark chocolate
6 eggs
tablespoon or two of red wine or brandy

You can jazz this superbly simple dish up a bit by putting little macaroons at the bottom of each glass and when the mousse sets, top off with thick cream.

Separate the eggs and whisk the whites until very stiff.

Melt the chocolate and add your alcohol.

Beat the egg yolks and pour in the melted chocolate. Mix together. Now add half the egg whites to the chocolate, mixing together gently. Then add the rest of the whites folding them in gently. Pour into glasses and refrigerate.

Maureen's Chocolate Galette

For the pastry:
7 oz. plain flour
1 oz. cocoa powder
5 oz. butter
3 oz. icing sugar
2 egg yolks, beaten

For the filling:
8 oz. butter
1 measure brandy
3 oz. cocoa powder
2 oz. icing sugar

For the covering:
1 block expensive dark chocolate
1 oz. butter
4 tablespoons milk

Make the pastry: mix the cocoa, flour and icing sugar together. Add the beaten eggs and knead in the butter. Leave to rest for one hour before rolling out. Divide into three 10" rounds about ⅛" thick – in other words, as thin as possible. Bake for 5 or 6 minutes at 200°C/400°F/gas 6. Leave to cool.

Now mix the filling ingredients together to make a rich chocolate butter cream. Spread the cream over the rounds to make a three-tiered sandwich. By now the whole thing is about ¾" in height.

Finally melt the dark chocolate with the butter and the milk and pour over the galette. If you like you could grate some hard chocolate over the whole thing when the top has set.

Index

Notes

Notes

Keith Floyd was born at Folly Farm, Reading, in 1943 and has held it responsible for his actions ever since. Educated at Wellington School in Somerset where, during the school holidays, he cooked for the first time when the mother of the family with whom he was staying fell ill and as a 12 year old was obliged to feed 5 hungry farmers for one long week.

On leaving school he became a journalist but the film 'Zulu' persuaded him to join the army resulting in his having to cook breakfast on a primus for a whole platoon on Dartmoor when the ration truck failed to bring the cooker. As a 2nd lieutenant in the Royal Tank Regiment he complained about the food and was promptly made 'messing member'.

After the army he spent his time travelling, getting work and experience in hotels and restaurants throughout the country. By 1971 he had 3 restaurants, a take-away, a film location catering service and a dial-a-dinner service all in the city of Bristol. In 1973 each of his 3 restaurants gained entries in that year's Good Food Guide!

Gradually becoming disillusioned with the British restaurant scene he sold out, bought a yacht and sailed for 2 years vowing never to run a restaurant again – during this time he opened restaurants in Spain and Portugal for friends. A Francophile of long standing he eventually moved to Provence and opened a restaurant in Isle-sur-la-Sorgue near Avignon, turning it into one of the leading restaurants in the area.

In his remarkable career Keith Floyd has opened 9 restaurants, the latest being in Chandos Road in Bristol. Due to prior commitments he has recently turned down his tenth restaurant – a château in Provence offered to him by friends.